Stacy and Steve

Pam Scheunemann

Consulting Editor, Diane Craig, M.A./Reading Specialist

ABDO
Publishing Company

Published by ABDO Publishing Company, 4940 Viking Drive, Edina, Minnesota 55435.

Printed in the United States.

Credits
Edited by: Pam Price
Curriculum Coordinator: Nancy Tuminelly
Cover and Interior Design and Production: Mighty Media
Child Photography: Steven Wewerka, Wewerka Photography
Photo Credits: AbleStock, Comstock, Photodisc

Library of Congress Cataloging-in-Publication Data

Scheunemann, Pam, 1955-
    Stacy and Steve / Pam Scheunemann.
        p. cm. -- (First sounds)
    Includes index.
    ISBN 1-59679-196-9 (hardcover)
    ISBN 1-59679-197-7 (paperback)
        1. English language--Consonants--Juvenile literature. I. Title. II. Series.
    PE1159.S344 2005
    428.1'3--dc22
                                                                                2004059503

SandCastle™ books are created by a professional team of educators, reading specialists, and content developers around five essential components that include phonemic awareness, phonics, vocabulary, text comprehension, and fluency. All books are written, reviewed, and leveled for guided reading, early intervention reading, and Accelerated Reader® programs and designed for use in shared, guided, and independent reading and writing activities to support a balanced approach to literacy instruction.

Let Us Know

After reading the book, SandCastle would like you to tell us your stories about reading. What is your favorite page? Was there something hard that you needed help with? Share the ups and downs of learning to read. We want to hear from you! To get posted on the ABDO Publishing Company Web site, send us e-mail at:

sandcastle@abdopub.com

SandCastle Level: Emerging

st

ABCDEFGH
IJKLMNOPQ
RSTUVWXYZ

abcdefgh
ijklmnopq
rstuvwxyz

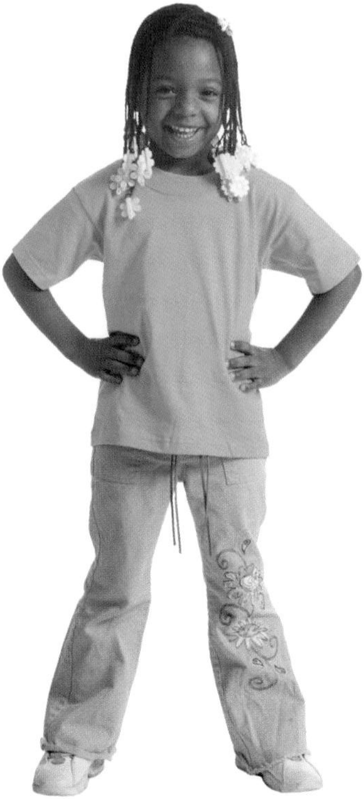

Stacy

Steve

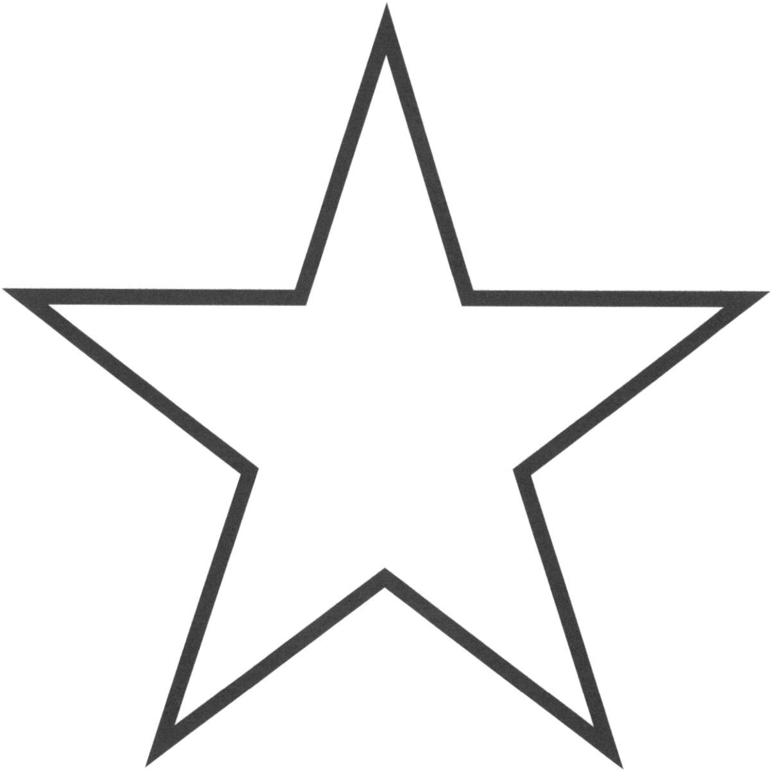

star

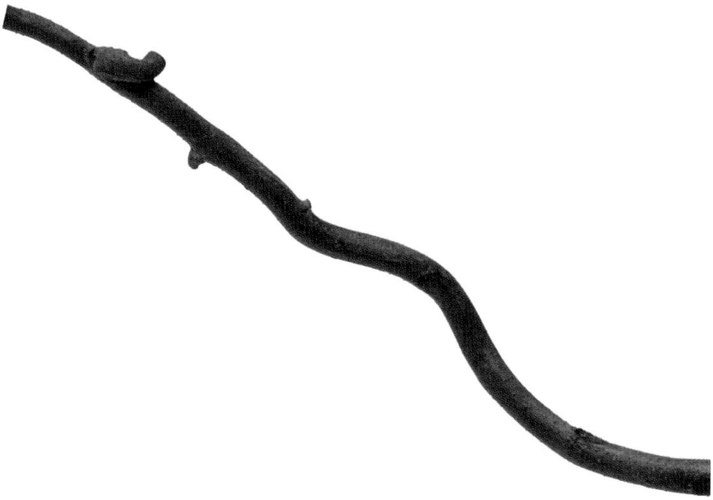

stick

strawberry

stove

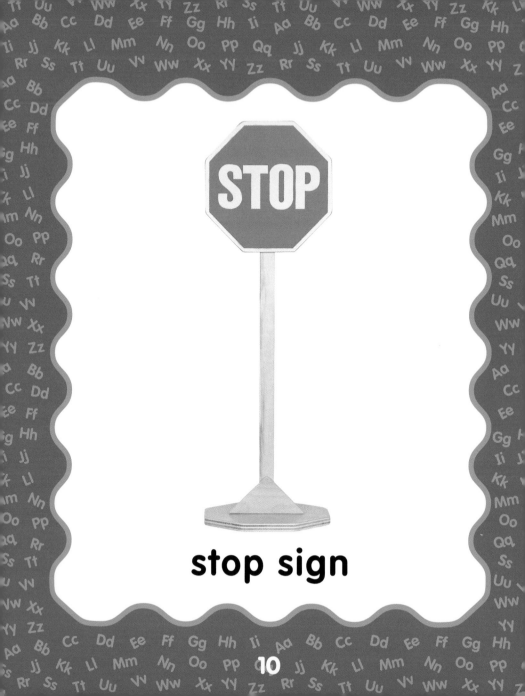

stop sign

The 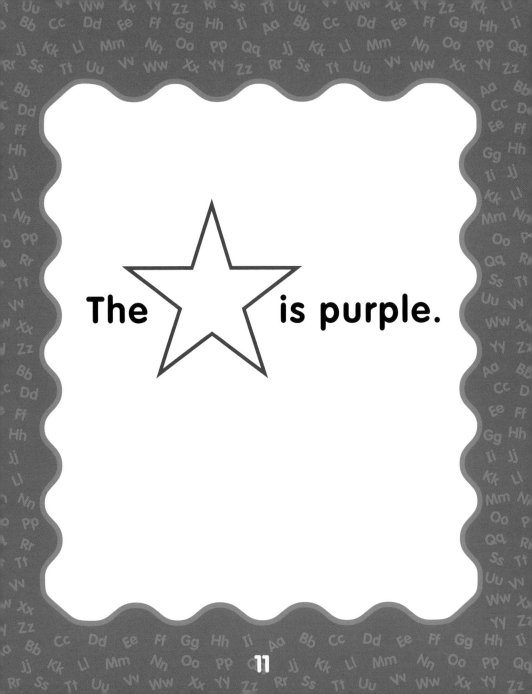 is purple.

The 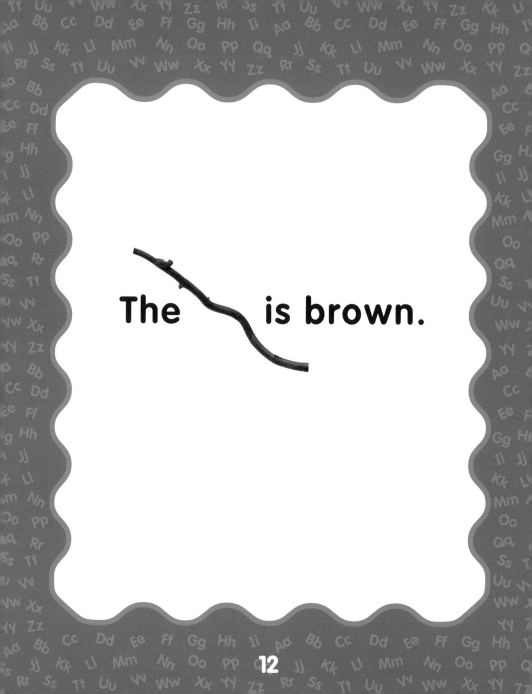 is brown.

Here is a  .

The  is white.

The 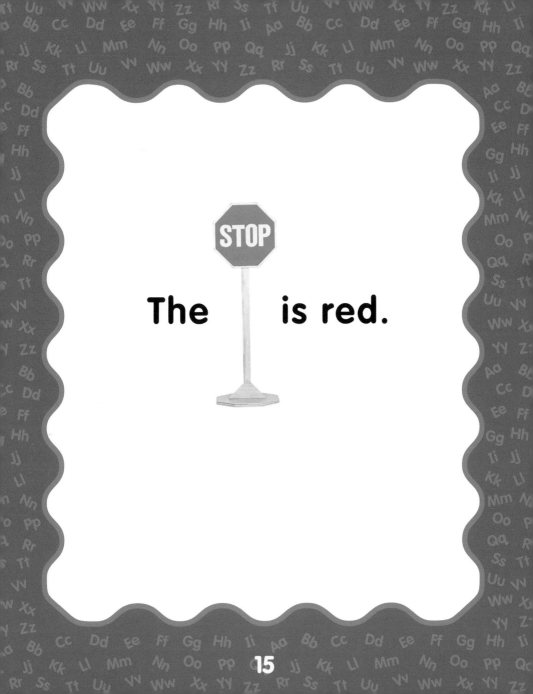 is red.

Stacy has a star.

Steve has a stick.

The star is on the stick.

Which of these pictures begin with st?

More words that begin with st

stand

start

step

sticker

stood

stool

store

story

About SandCastle™

A professional team of educators, reading specialists, and content developers created the SandCastle™ series to support young readers as they develop reading skills and strategies and increase their general knowledge. The SandCastle™ series has four levels that correspond to early literacy development in young children. The levels are provided to help teachers and parents select the appropriate books for young readers.

Emerging Readers
(no flags)

Beginning Readers
(1 flag)

Transitional Readers
(2 flags)

Fluent Readers
(3 flags)

These levels are meant only as a guide. All levels are subject to change.

To see a complete list of SandCastle™ books and other nonfiction titles from ABDO Publishing Company, visit www.abdopub.com or contact us at:
4940 Viking Drive, Edina, Minnesota 55435 • 1-800-800-1312 • fax: 1-952-831-1632